NICKELODEON

Zoey 101™

Perfect Parties,
Sleepovers & more!

Perfect Parties, Sleepovers & more!

By Jo Hurley
Scholastic Inc.

ISBN-13: 978-0-439-88976-6
ISBN-10: 0-439-88976-6
© 2007 ApolloMedia.
Published by Scholastic Inc.
SCHOLASTIC and associated logos are trademarks and/or registered trademarks of Scholastic Inc.
12 11 10 9 8 7 6 5 4 3 2 1   7 8 9 10 11/0
Printed in China.
First printing, March 2007

SCHOLASTIC INC.

New York   Toronto   London   Aukland   Sydney
Mexico City   New Delhi   Hong Kong   Buenos Aires

Now Entering the Party Zone

A Word from Zoey

What's shaking, Stingrays?

Are you in the mood for some seriously crazy fun and absolutely NO SLEEP? Lola, Quinn, and I have been thinking hard about how to host the ultimate, one-of-a-kind, major sleepover. So here's what we came up with.

First things first: Slumber parties are better when there are no boys allowed. Not that we don't love hanging with Chase or Michael, but the fact is that when the guys are around, you can't really do girl stuff like beauty make-overs and gossip. And that is the whole reason we're here, right? I mean, we're the first girls at an all-boy school. We make up our own rules.

Speaking of rules, your party needs 'em. Even though slumber parties are mostly parent-free, there needs to be a real party policy. Things like: Don't talk so loudly, no running upstairs, and no pranks, please. Agree (with an adult) on what these rules will be ahead of time. Plus, make secret code words to secretly warn a grown-up if you need her or him during the party.

Most essential thing: Have a B-L-A-S-T. There's no point in having a sleepover if you don't kick loose, right? Let yourself be made over with frizzy hair and green eye shadow. Get messy. Dish on all the grooviest gossip. Have the night of your life.

See u after the party, friends!

Zo'

Zoey's Top 5 "Must Have" Slumber Party Essentials

1. PILLOWS — lots of them. How else will you have a great pillow fight before the night is through?

2. CAMERA. Digital is great, natch, because you can e-mail pics at the end of the party or print them out on your computer. Video cams are cool, too. But why not buy a few disposable cameras, too? Have them on hand throughout the party for some killer candids. . . .

3. OVER-SIZE WHITE T-SHIRTS AND FABRIC MARKERS. Sign on the shirt — anywhere.

4. SNACK SUPPLIES. To munch or not to munch? What kind of question is that? Slumber parties are the BEST place to pig out with your girlfriends. Pick healthier snacks like trail mix and dried fruit whenever possible.

5. "GET THIS PARTY STARTED" MUSIC MIX — burn a CD with all the fave tunes of you and your party guests. Nothing gets a sleepover rolling like some good music.

Get Your Party Started.

Here's a short list of all the things you need to do.

#1 MAKE YOUR GUEST LIST

You want to have a party, so what's the occasion? Birthday bash? Summer night? Bon voyage? Think hard before you invite friends. *You don't want anyone to feel left out.*

#2 CHOOSE A THEME

The most important task you have is to pick your party theme. Keep in mind the likes and dislikes of all your guests. *See pages 6 and 7 for theme suggestions.*

#3 DESIGN YOUR INVITATIONS

Ask guests to bring sleeping bag, pillow, PJs, slippers or sox, toothbrush, and whatever extras they need (based on your theme). Keep extra stuff on hand in case someone forgets to bring one of their items.

> **Key information to include on your invite:**
> - Name of Party (and Theme)
> - Host of Party
> - Address and Phone
> - Date and Time of Party (don't forget to include drop-off and pick-up times)
> - RSVP phone number or e-mail
> - Request for what to bring to party (i.e., pillow, sleeping bag, T-shirt, etc.)

4

#4 DECORATE THE PLACE

Props, posters, flowers, signs, and more can dress up the place — and put you and your guests in the best party mood. Colored lights, glow-in-the-dark stickers, and mood music ALL make a big difference.

#5 SELECT YOUR MENU

What fun is a party without the right snacks? Will you be serving dinner and breakfast? Put some planning into the menu. Let your guests help make the food — and clean up, too, of course.

#6 PLAN FUN ACTIVITIES

Don't host a party without a game plan. Whether it is board games or beauty products you'll need, be prepared. Make lists of stuff ahead of time and double-check your supplies the day before the party.

#7 PASS OUT FAVORS AND PRIZES

Have goody bags so that everyone who leaves the party in the A.M. has a memento of the occasion.

Slumber Party Dream Themes

The Official PCA List*

1. SPA-TACULAR
Transform your party into a total spa when you give each other mega-makeovers with fun facials, creative pedicures, new 'dos, and more.
See pages 8 - 13

2. SCAREDY-CATS
Who's afraid of the dark? Turn an ordinary party into a ghost party! Tell spooky tales and see who gets (and gives) the most goose bumps.
See pages 14 - 17

3. TIME WARP
Take a step back in time with a groovy costume party. Have guests dress in tie-dye or poodle skirts when you choose another era as your party setting.
See pages 18 - 21

4. TUNE OUT
A star is born! Invite party guests to come with sleeping bags — and a song. Step up to the microphone and lip-synch, make a music video, or just play your favorite tunes and dance around.
See pages 22 - 25

5. ARTY PARTY
Your party will be colorific when you turn your living room into a picture gallery. Paint, draw, make collages, decorate T-shirts, and put the "arty" back in "party."
See pages 26 - 29

6. CASTAWAY
See the planet — without ever leaving your house. Ask party guests to come dressed in the clothes of their favorite international destination. Serve food and play games inspired by that place.
See pages 30 - 31

7. SHE'S GOT GAME
Who has time to slumber? From flashlight tag to Twister, there's plenty to cheer about when you host an on-the-move sports party.
See pages 32 - 35

8. PILLOW TALK
Sometimes gossip makes the best sleepover activity. Mellow out with lots of gab, good snacks, games like Truth or Dare, and classic friendship movies.
See pages 36 - 39

* These party themes have been tried and tested by the PCA crew, including Zoey, Nic, Quinn, and Lola. And they Joooooved 'em! Here's hoping you will, too. . . .

7

Spa-Tacular

Invite Ideas

Bar of soap shape — or attach to a real bar of soap or mini bottle of lotion.

Make a fake Mirror, Mirror (using cardstock, pastel-colored paper, markers, aluminum foil) — and print the words on the back.

Use "beauty shop" lingo. Invite friends to "drop into your salon," and call the party start time an "appointment with beauty."

Make sure you ask each guest to bring her own towel and hairbrush, along with any other beauty supplies she loves.

Decorations

- Make sure you set up your party in a room with electrical outlets for hair dryers, beauty equipment, and whatever else you may need to plug in.

- Pick a party room near a bathroom so you can duck into the sink and check the mirror often.

- Tack up pictures torn from magazines — for ideas and inspiration.

- Set up beauty "stations" for nails and hair. Use card tables covered with cute pink paper tablecloths and centerpieces.

Remember to use hypoallergenic stuff so no one breaks out in a rash or hives.

Try sponge curlers instead of hot curling irons; they're safer. . . .

Don't fall asleep until the makeup comes off your face! Use alcohol-free toner or cold cream to take it off.

Supplies

- Shampoo and conditioner
- Styling gel or hair spray
- Coated rubber bands, bobby pins, barrettes
- Cleansing soap
- Cornstarch and aloe powder
- Makeup: shadow, blush, mascara, lipstick, lip gloss
- Emery boards, nail clippers
- Nail polish (assorted colors)
- Nail polish remover
- Cotton wedges, cotton balls, Q-tips

Ask friends to bring their own — or supply the stuff you want. This is only a starter list. Get more ideas from beauty magazines.

9

Spa-Tacular

Try thinly sliced cucumbers or cold cuts on crust-free bread.

Put out a pitcher of water with slices of lemon and ice cubes.

Food

- Since this party's all about looking good, you probably want to be cooking good, too. Make way for healthier snacks like carrots and hummus (chickpea dip) or cut-up apples with peanut butter.

- The finest salons serve food fit for a princess. So should you!

Satisfy your sweet tooth with miniature oatmeal cookies, licorice sticks, or green grapes.

Get takeout from Sushi Rox! Okay, this only really works at PCA, but you could pretend you're there, right? Right!

NO-PEEKING MAKEOVER

This can be done two different ways.

1. Guests (and you) can do self-makeovers using all kinds of makeup colors and styles — but without looking. Set a timer for ten minutes and see who can do the best "face" without ever glancing in a mirror.

2. Pair up and make over each other — but with a catch: The person doing the makeover must wear a blindfold. Set the timer for an agreed-upon time limit (10 or 15 minutes is usually enough) and then start your makeover engines. Who's got lipstick on her chin? This works even better (with funnier results) if you blindfold the person who is doing someone else's hair, too.

Goody Bag Idea!
Clear baggies filled with before and after photos from the makeover, sample-size bottles of glitter polish, temporary tattoos, and press-on nails.

11

Now You're Stylin'

FANCY FRENCH TWISTS

YOU NEED:
styling gel
bobby pins
hair spray

Gather medium shoulder-length hair into a ponytail at your neck and put in lots of styling gel.

Now, twist hair with hand and continue twisting until the roll is tight. Stick in the loose ends and use bobby pins to secure the twist.

Mist with hair spray when done. Want extra sparkle in your twist? Mix in fine glitter with light-hold styling gel for a super-shimmery look.

SPIKES

YOU NEED:
1 envelope unflavored gelatin
¼ cup hot water (to dissolve gelatin), hair spray

Hair that's 4–5 inches long or less can stand up on its own for a punk look. In small bowl, mix gelatin and water and wait for it to thicken and cool off. Slick the mix into your hair like you would do with styling gel. Shape your spikes however you like best and then spritz with hair spray so it stays put.

Warning: Hair Don't!

Some sources say you can use Kool-Aid to temporarily dye your hair. But beware! The color may not come out for several washings. Stay safe when you redo hairdos. Use gels and sprays that easily wash out with shampoo and conditioner.

Fun ideas for hair makeovers you and your friends can do to each other!

RIBBON BRAIDS

YOU NEED:
assortment of long,
colorful, thin ribbons
covered hair elastics

Get streaks of color in your
hair — by using ribbons instead
of dye! This works best for long
hair. Grab a handful of hair and
divide into three sections.
Starting right at your scalp (at
the roots), wrap one of your
ribbons around the whole length
of one section of the hair. Then
braid the three together so
the ribbon is now intertwined
into the center of the braid.
Secure at bottom with the
elastic. Create numerous different thin braids all over your
head for a groovy look.

Scaredy-Cats

Invite Ideas

Write to your guests in a spooky tone like, "I Dare You to Come to My Sleepover . . ." and "Are you brave enough to survive a night . . ." or "Be prepared to be scared silly!"

Craft your invitation on black or dark-blue colored paper, write the words in colored gel pen, and stuff miniature plastic ants or spiders in the envelope for an extra scare.

For the words on your invite, cut out letters and words from a magazine and paste them onto paper like a ransom note.

14

- Anything you'd put out for Halloween can come out for this sleepover, too: fake bugs, fake hands with fake blood, spooky music or sound effects, door signs that read **Beware** or **Enter at Your Own Risk** or **Turn Back Now — Or Else!**

- Dress doorways and mirrors in fake cobwebs.

- Put black lightbulbs into ordinary lamps.

- Make one section of your room like a makeshift graveyard with funny tombstones.

- Turn your basement, attic, or any part of your house into a haunted mansion. Get Mom, Dad, or your siblings to help out with the scares (and screams!).

Supplies

- Flashlights for everyone so no one is ever really in the dark

- Five-minute-mystery books so you can read together and take turns being detectives

Scaredy-Cats

Food

- Worm Explosion (Spaghetti with sauce)

- Shake Your Guts (Jell-O with gummy worms inside)

- There's a Bug in My Juice! (Fruit punch with fly ice cubes)

- Mud Monster Cake (Chocolate cake with oozy icing)

> **Label all your snacks and meals with gross, scary, and funny names!**

Things to Do

- Read scary stories aloud to each other! One of the best collections is *Scary Stories* by Alvin Schwartz, which includes some classic folklore nail-biters and urban legends. You can also check out short stories by Edgar Allan Poe (classic horror), Stephen King (modern horror), or Ray Bradbury (more science fiction.)

- Go around the room and make up your own scary short story.

- Play Killer, the great winking game.

PCA

Monsterrific DVDs

Nothing says scary like sitting in the dark with a squeaking door, howling wind, and a spooktacular flick on your TV set. Huddle close and watch some of these scary (and funny) movies. . . .

- **Monster Squad**
- **Goonies**
- **Ghostbusters**
- **Gremlins**
- **Beetlejuice**
- **The Haunted Mansion**
- **The Birds**
- **The Blob**

Hint: You can also go for something with dark, kitschy appeal like the original, black-and-white Frankenstein or Dracula.

Remember: Not everyone likes horror flicks, so ask for help to choose the right movie for everyone.

Time Warp

Plan your party for another generation. Travel back in time to the 1950s, 1960s, or 1970s with costumes, music, food, and games from that time. Groovy!

Invite Ideas

Create a fifties invitation that looks like a record album. Use cardboard and colored markers; poke a center hole like a real album; and write the details in the circle.

Make a sixties flower power invitation, using flowered wrapping paper or your own painted flower design.

Make your seventies invitation in the shape of a disco ball, using foil stickers and neon pens.

- For the fifties, turn your room into a sock hop; and hang up assorted socks on the walls.

- For the sixties, hang strands of beads or put out lava lamps.

- For the seventies, hang silver streamers or get a pulsing strobe light.

Supplies

- Crazy straws
- Hula hoops
- Bubble blowers

Food

- **BING BONGS** (okay, so maybe these are only available at PCA, but it's your job to find a good substitute like maybe . . . vanilla frosted cupcakes with little cinnamon candies on 'em?)

- **PIGS-IN-BLANKETS** (Get the frozen kind and microwave when you're ready to eat.)

- **SUPERTHICK MILKSHAKES** (Mix together vanilla and chocolate ice cream and chocolate syrup for a super-yummy treat.)

- **RICE KRISPIE SQUARES** (Look for the best recipe on the cereal box.)

Things to Do

- Host a hula hoop contest in your living room or backyard. Who can keep her hoop spinning the longest?

- Face painting. Use hypoallergenic makeup to decorate one another's faces with rainbows, peace symbols, and stars.

Make Trendy, Tie-dyed Stuff*

Carefully Read Instructions on Package of Dye

YOU NEED:
White, 100 percent cotton T-shirt
Thick rubber bands
Thick rubber gloves
1/2 cup liquid dye
(or 1 package powdered dye)
for each color you want to use
1 cup hot water
5 tablespoons salt
Container for dye

*Translation:
shirts, napkins, pillowcases, socks, or whatever else you think would look good

1. Wet your T-shirt (or whatever you're dying). Now place the wet shirt flat on your work surface.

2. Tie knots in the T-shirt, or twist and secure folds with the thick rubber bands.

3. Mix dye in hot water. Dissolve salt in the mixture and let the mixture cool to room temperature.

4. Put on your gloves and place shirt in the dye. If you want the entire shirt to be one color, then go ahead and dunk it. If you want different colors, then dunk one section at a time.

5. After dunking, rinse the shirt in cold water until the water runs clear.

6. Undo the knots and rinse the shirt again.

7. Hang the shirt to dry, out of the sun. But be careful each time you wash. Colors may run.

21

Tune Out

Be sure to invite friends with the right lingo. Instead of "You're Invited" put "Calling All Superstars!"

Copy plain sheet music with the invitation's words on the staffs. Try and make your invite rhyme like a pop song.

Make stamps of musical notes and stamp colorful cardstock with your own medley of notes and lyrics.

Decorations

- Copy plain sheet music with the invitation's words on the staffs. Try and make your invite rhyme like a pop song.

- Turn your house into a dance studio for the party. Cut out giant musical notes and tape them to the wall and mirrors.

- During the party, leave your TV on a channel like VH-1 showing music videos all the time.

- Provide plastic starworthy sunglasses as goodies for all of your guests. You can pick up cheap plastic ones in bright colors at a local party store.

- Don't forget your stage! Set up one special area of your living room or bedroom especially for the performances. Spread a blanket on the floor and make room for the audience, too.

Food

What's a musical performance without a snack? Make personalized popcorn in honor of your favorite PCA character. Pop (or microwave) the corn and then sprinkle on or add the extra, zippy ingredients.

- Add cinnamon and sugar . . . soooo sweet, like Zoey!

- Add butter and parmesan cheese . . . tangy like Nicole!

- Add peanuts, raisins, corn nuts, and mini chocolate chips . . . inventive like Quinn!

PCA POPCORN

Things to Do

- Write and perform your own rap song as a group.

- Play Music Trivia. Try to name all the members of a favorite (or obscure) band or fill in the lyrics to a favorite song. To find the correct lyrics, surf the Net and use a search engine.

- Lip-Synch like crazy! Put on your favorite discs, grab a pretend microphone, and sing your heart out. Can you copy the mega–moves of your singing idol?

AND NOW FOR SOMETHING COMPLETELY DIFFERENT!

Instead of settling for one prize when you win the trivia test or some other sleepover game, why not get a choice of prizes? Beware: Not all prizes in the boxes are good ones. It's based on the old game show *Let's Make a Deal*.

YOU NEED:

3 shoeboxes and assorted prizes (both good ones and clunkers!)

• SUGGESTED GOOD PRIZES:

mini bottles of nail polish, ribbons, movie passes, video rental passes, bouncy balls, candy, stuffed animals, pencils and pens, playing cards or trading cards, paperback books

• SUGGESTED CLUNKER PRIZES:

rocks, twigs, paper cups

WHAT TO DO:

Put prizes into the three boxes. Players try to guess which box has the best prize. When they choose, they can either "trade it" for another box (and, hopefully, better prizes) or "keep it." Try to make sure that all party guests get at least one great prize.

Make Your Own Music Video
By Zoey

1. Borrow the best video camera in your neighborhood. Take no chances when making a masterpiece. And make sure it's charged before you get going.

2. Pick a fun song and make sure the singer knows all the words.

3. Burn your music video song onto a CD so you can listen to it a lot.

4. Write a very short script.

5. Create a list of shots to be staged. Something like: "Stand up, twirl around, flip hair, and jump into the air while singing song." Write down the settings for each staged shot: kitchen, porch, bedroom, etc.

6. Review ideas and take turns suggesting how shots could also be filmed.

7. Practice your entire "shoot" without a camera first. Then, turn on the camera and . . .

8. You're ready to roll! Next stop: MTV Music Video Awards. Oh, wow, what will we wear on the red carpet? Seriously, though, you need a video premiere, so have all the guests sit down to watch the first screening of your masterpiece!

Music Video Lingo
- **Wide shot:** something that shows the entire group and set
- **Medium shot:** putting the camera on wide shot and then close-up and back again
- **Close-up:** zooming in on just one singer
- **Changing the angle:** moving the camera and yourself to capture different angles on your subject
- **Lighting:** Be sure bright lights shine from behind you, directly on the performer faces.

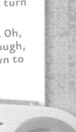

25

Cut out paper in the shape of an easel or a paint palette and print the party information on the back.

Send a black-and-white invitation along with a few crayons.

Decorations

• Hang butcher paper along one wall. You can use this throughout the party to paint or draw a giant party mural.

• String up different colored streamers around the room.

• Make flowers from pipe cleaners and tissue paper and use for centerpieces on your art tables.

• Cut out fake posterboard "frames" (measuring 11" x 17" or bigger). Don't forget to leave the center empty — the art is yet to come! On the bottom part of each fake frame, attach a label with a party guest's name. Once the guest arrives, it's her job to make an art masterpiece for that frame at some point during the party.

Food

Supplies

PAINTED TOAST

Line up five paper cups and fill with approximately 2–3 tablespoons of milk. Drop food coloring into each cup. Mix colors and, using ordinary (clean!) paintbrushes, paint a slice of white bread with stripes, stars, or a pretty picture. Toss the slices into the toaster and *voilá* . . . sandwich art!

ICE-CREAM SUNDAE ART

Invite friends to decorate ice-cream sundaes with as many creative — and colorful — items as possible. Put out dishes with sauces (cherry, hot fudge, butterscotch). Sample crunchy toppings, too: raisins, M&M's, gummy bears, colored sprinkles, and more. Mix red or blue food coloring into Cool Whip to top it off.

GOO POPS

Zoey loves these sweet frozen treats . . . which somehow melt all over everything if you're not careful. But hey, maybe melted Goo Pop is a good thing? It can double as paint for your art project! *Hint: For this party snack, any brightly colored Popsicle will do.*

- Paper aprons for each guest
- Paintbrushes
- Plastic cups
- Little watercolor sets
- Glue sticks (or white glue)
- Pairs of scissors
- Glitter, sequins, feathers, felt, or other craft items
- Magic Markers and crayons

- **PAINT YOUR OWN POTTERY.**
  Buy unpainted, inexpensive pottery
  plates or pots, along with a set of
  pottery paints. Paint with original
  designs. After the party, have the
  plates fired at a pottery shop.

- **DECORATE PLAIN T-SHIRTS.** Create
  original designs using colored fabric
  markers, fabric glue, or puffy paint. Have
  guests sign the shirts with indelible
  marker once they've been designed.

- **HOST A CARICATURE CONTEST.** First,
  give every party guest a pencil and
  sketch pad. Then, put every guest's name
  into a hat. Have guests select a name at
  random — and keep it secret. For the
  next twenty minutes, have guests draw
  the person whose name she picked.
  When portraits are done, show off
  the results. Who can guess
  who's who?

DESIGNS BY ZOEY

28

Friendship Bracelets (or Anklets)

Make homemade letter beads and string them together as a token of your undying devotion to your best buds. Spell out favorite text messages or secret crush names. It's the ultimate sleepover keepsake.

Heads Up: You need to make the beads and let them dry a few days before your party.

HOMEMADE LETTER BEADS

YOU NEED:
- 2 cups flour
- 1/2 cup salt
- 3/4 cup water
- 1 tablespoon vegetable oil
- Assorted toothpicks
- Tempura paint and brush
- String or thread (strong is best)
- Newspaper

HERE'S WHAT TO DO:
1. Mix flour, salt, water, and cooking oil in bowl and knead for 5 minutes.
2. Shape the dough into funky bead shapes (circles, squares, hot dog shape).
3. Poke a hole through each bead with a toothpick, leaving enough room for string or thread to pass through.
4. Let beads air dry on a sheet of newspaper for at least 2 days.
5. Then, paint the beads with colored designs and letters.

Have Your Jewelry — And Eat It, Too!
Not enough time to make homemade beads? Make edible jewelry using very thin licorice (for string), Fruit Loops, Cheerios, Life Savers, and other candies with holes in the center. Jewelry and a snack all in one? Sounds like the perfect Quinnvention, right?

Castaway

Invite Ideas

Put invitation on the back of a palm tree postcard in 3-D. Along the bottom of the card, affix glue and sand — and mail in envelope with a miniature paper umbrella.

Start the invite by saying, "Get Lost with Me! Pack Your Bag and Set Sail for an Island Adventure."

Decorations

- Pick up old travel posters from a local travel agency.

- Cut out pictures from travel magazines or *National Geographic*.

- Hang up colorful flags, put out beach towels, hang "fake" palm fronds made from construction paper.

- Put up pretend tiki torches (just like the ones on *Survivor*) and wooden idols.

30

- BBQ chicken, plain or on pizza
- Tropical fruit salad: mango, Ugli fruit, pineapple, banana
- Mixed snack bowls with different flavored Goldfish crackers

- Instead of sleeping in the living room, asleep out under the stars. If it's a warm spring night or summertime, pitch a tent in the backyard. Don't forget the mosquito repellent!

- Looking for a *Survivor*-style challenge — with rewards? Plan a Super Scavenger Hunt! Give everyone a "treasure map," which is really just a list of things to find. The first person to find the most objects wins a special prize! Some of the items you can put on your list: greeting card, juice box, gumball, pair of sneakers, umbrella, newspaper, etc. *Here's a tip: Give each guest her list in a sealed envelope and make her start in a different room in your house. That way, not everyone will rush for the same items at once.*

Bonus Ideas!
- *Bring your scavenger hunt outside at night! Give everyone a flashlight and ask them to find objects and items in the dark.*

- *Put the scavenger hunt list/clues into CODE. Scramble words so it makes finding the stuff trickier.*

31

She's Got Game

Create Olympic-medal invitations using large circles, gold paint, and fancy lettering.

Write invitations or instructions on uninflated balloons. They need to be inflated to be read!

Supplies

- Decide ahead of time what games you want to play: basketball, soccer, or maybe croquet? Make sure you have all equipment on hand.

- Wipe-off board and dry erase markers to keep scores

- Stopwatch

- Don't forget: If you're exercising or playing sports, you should prepare for accidents. Keep Band-Aids, antibiotic cream, instant ice packs, and other first aid supplies nearby.

Decorations

Turn your living room into an Olympic stadium with flags, signs, and posters of athletes.

Food

- Pretend you're at an athletic event and serve bottled water, Gatorade, orange slices, granola bars, etc.

- Think red, white, and blue: vanilla ice cream topped with strawberries and blueberries. Or, for breakfast the morning after the party, serve pancakes or waffles with the same topping.

- Make a salad bar with regular selections like lettuce, tomato, and sliced peppers. But add interesting items like shredded cheese, sunflower seeds or walnuts, chunks of apple, and more.

#1

She's Got Game

Things to Do

• **SLEEPING BAG RACES (OR PILLOW CASE RACES)** — Hop in and see who can get from spot A to spot B the fastest.

• **FLASHLIGHT TAG** — everyone plays outside to see who can hide (and run) the best.

• **BLINDFOLDED RACES** — the old standard game for parties! Line up and see who can carry an egg on a spoon across the room.

Eyes on the Prize
If everything's a contest, then you need prizes. Purchase red, white, and blue ribbons or gold foil candies for contest winners. Don't limit prizes to the athletic events, either. Why not give awards for funny stuff like Messiest Eater, Loudest Snorer, Party Pooper, Best Joker, and more?

Sleeping Bag Obstacle Course

YOU NEED:
- At least 4 players
- A relatively open area like your backyard (lawn) or your carpeted living room floor
- Sleeping bags
- 3 or more empty 2-liter soda bottles

HERE'S WHAT YOU DO:
- Divide the group into teams. Each team gets one sleeping bag. Set up a course by putting soda bottles in different locations.

- On the word "go," the first players of each team get into their sleeping bags and wiggle around the bottles. *(It works best if players hold the sleeping bag with their hands and use their arms and elbows to help them crawl.)*

- When players get back to their team, they tag the next person in line. The first team to finish wins.

MIX IT UP
- You don't have to do an obstacle course with sleeping bags, but the game works best with some handicap, like having your shoelaces tied together or not being able to use your hands.

- You could fill your course with outrageous tasks like rolling a hard-boiled egg with your nose, shimmying across the floor with a balloon or ball between your knees, being blindfolded, or hopping the entire time.

Pillow Talk

Print invitations on pink paper cut out like a pillowcase — with lace or ribbon glued around the edge.

Make an invitation that looks like a sleeping bag. Inside, slip in another homemade item: a paper doll!

Cut out stars and moons and string them together like a night sky. Put your celestial invite into a deep-blue envelope addressed with a gold marker and star stickers.

- Mylar balloons in the shape of stars and moons, or round silver and gold balloons (like the planets). Hang up anything to make the room look like a starry sky.

- Pillow, pillows everywhere! The key to this party is pillows and comfort . . . except when you're having pillow fights, of course.

While you're gossiping, you keep on munching! Put out bowls of chips, pretzels, sesame sticks, or raw vegetables. Check out the recipe below.

TO-DIE-FOR DIP YOU NEED:
- 1/2 cup light mayonnaise
- 1 1/2 cups light sour cream
- 3 tablespoons minced onion
- 1 tablespoon dried dill
- 1 teaspoon garlic salt

HERE'S WHAT TO DO:
- Mix ingredients together at least one hour before your party starts. Keep in refrigerator to chill.

- Serve with cut-up, raw veggies (celery, carrots, red pepper, radishes, cucumber, cherry tomato, or broccoli).

Things to Do

- **FRIENDSHIP GAME CIRCLE**
  Everyone on the floor! Grab a pillow and prepare to DISH. A sleepover just wouldn't be a sleepover without some of these games:

- **CONFESS OR STRESS**
  Play it like your PCA pals! You need a pair of dice and a willingness to admit your most horrible experiences out loud. Roll the dice to see if you have to confess something embarrassing or take a dare. What can you dream up?

- **I NEVER**
  Get your buddies to admit their secret crushes by admitting your own! Start by saying something like, "I never thought Logan Reese was cute." If anyone else in the group thought that was true for her, even just once, even just for ten seconds, she has to put up her hand and admit it!

More Movies!
Here are some other movies that make good company at a slumber party. Warning: Some scenes may have a high "friend" factor. While watching, box of tissues and some major hugs may be needed.

- *A Little Princess*
- *Clueless*
- *Ever After*
- *Harriet the Spy*
- *Homeward Bound*
- *Never Been Kissed*
- *The Parent Trap*
- *The Princess Bride*
- *The Secret Garden*
- *Stand by Me*
- *Toy Story 1 & 2*

DREAM BOX ZOEY

Keepsake Boxes

YOU NEED:
- Little cardboard or wooden box (available at craft supply shops)
- Glittery or metallic paint and paintbrushes
- Old magazines
- White glue or a stronger sealer product
- Scissors

HERE'S WHAT TO DO:
- Paint the top of your box with the glitter paint.

- While waiting for the paint to dry, clip out teeny photos and words from magazines. Give yourself a theme for each box: friendship, summer, sleep, or something else fun.

- Glue down the miniature pictures and words. Overlap so everything fits together nicely.

- Put a small amount of white glue in a shallow dish or cup and add water. Stir together until it is a thin paste.

- Apply watered-down glue all over the collage. This should help to seal and protect your design! When you're done, compare boxes. Maybe you want to swap 'em before the slumber party ends.

Friendship Fill-ins

Here's a simple questionnaire for you and your sleepover pals to fill in and talk about together.

Do it in these E-Z steps:

- Try to make a copy of these fill-in pages for everyone or (if you can't get to a copy machine) have everyone write down her answers on a blank piece of paper.

- Play some funky music while all the sleepover pals fill in their answers. Ask everyone to fold her questionnaire and put those into a hat or box.

- Pick out one of the papers and read the answers aloud. Can anyone guess who's who?

1. Name _____

2. These are my favorites:

Color _____	Ice Cream _____
Snack _____	Drink _____
Time of Day _____	Class _____
Sport _____	Teacher _____
Singer _____	Song _____
Movie Star _____	Movie _____
Book _____	Magazine _____

3. The coolest person in my life is _____

   because _____

4. This makes me happy: _____

5. This makes me sad: _____

6. The most embarrassing thing that ever happened to me was:

   _____

   _____

7. The luckiest thing that ever happened to me was: _____

   _____

8. When I get older, I want to be: _____

   _____

9. If I could travel anywhere in the world, I'd go to: _____

   _____

10. If I had three magic wishes, I'd wish for:

   (1) _____

   (2) _____

   (3) _____

   Bonus: I can see into the future. I predict the following (insert one

   fortune for each of the sleepover guests):

   _____

   _____

   _____

   _____

Slumber Party Time Capsule

The best way to keep and preserve memories from your big party is to store 'em in a safe place like a time capsule. Remember when Mr. Bender helped Zoey and her friends to make their own capsule? Everyone put in something that would show off his or her personal style. Now you can do the same thing!

YOU NEED:
- Large coffee can
- Construction paper
- Paints and paint brushes
- Glue
- Plastic bags (quart or gallon sizes)
- Assorted items (see below)

Do Not Open Until
June 2020

HOW TO MAKE IT:
1. Use paint and/or construction paper to decorate the outside of the coffee can. Make a special design to commemorate your friendships and the sleepover. Maybe you can draw cartoons of each party guest or glue photos from the party?

2. Label the outside of the can with the date. If you plan to open it together in the future, then include that date, too. For example, Do Not Open Until June 2020.

3. For the inside of the can, include personal messages from each guest. You can write individual letters or a joint letter signed by everyone.

4. Copy down the questions from the friendship fill-ins on pages 40–41 and insert that into the capsule, too. Put all notes and paper into one of the plastic bags.

5. Toss in some personal items, too, like more photos, stories from the newspaper, or a CD of your favorite song. Can you come up with any other fun ideas? Put these into one or more plastic bags, too.

Why not choose a future date when you can open the capsule together and see if any of your predictions came true?

6. Seal the capsule. If the coffee can has a plastic lid, then glue the edges to seal it, or tape it shut.

7. Decide who will be "keeper of the capsule" or agree upon a place to hide it together. Some good places: Bury it in the backyard or hide it in the attic. Thanks to the plastic bags, your contents should be kept safe from moisture. Good luck!

2009 2010 2011

43

Keepsakes, Memories, and Scrapbooks

Don't let your slumber party pass without making a picture memento that will last a lifetime. Take lots of photos — and download them right away. Share them with party guests via e-mail as soon as possible. Then, make a Paper Bag Photo Book. Here's how.

1. Use 10 plain brown lunch bags.

2. Alternating the ends, put the bags together in a neat pile.

3. Fold the pile in half. The fold line is your "book" binding.

4. Poke holes into the binding, or spine. Use a scrapbooking tool to do this, or, use the sharp end of a scissor. Be extra-careful, please!

ZOEY

PCA GIRLS RULE!

When you make this mini scrapbook, you'll end up with more than one secret compartment to store extra photos and pictures. The folded ends of the bag are sometimes closed, but other times they make nifty pockets.

5. Choose your binding material. Long, colored ribbon works nicely. You can also try metal binding clips (available at a local office supply store).

6. Remember: This album is not acid-free, so the quality of the photos and the paper will get yellow or damaged over time.

Quinn

Lola

So Many Games, So Little Time!

Use these blank spaces to write down all you've done — and all that you have left to do before the big P-Day, as in Party Day.

46

T O S U R I O W Z

X A C D B g o a L n m P

P P J L H e K S P P A U

V W D C K B g a n

m o W P I K C D B a g

g a 9 A P I L

The Last Word
By Zoey Brooks

Ta-da! So, you are totally on your way to having an amazing fiesta! How cool is that?

There's one last thing I almost forgot to tell you. At any slumber party, you never, EVER want to run out of stuff to talk about. I know this book has a ton of ideas, but I figured that maybe I could give you just a few more topics of conversation. If I've learned anything at PCA, it's that you can never be too prepared.

- Should friends share all their thoughts — or is it okay to keep some secrets?

- Do you believe in aliens?

- What would you do if you won the lottery?

- Is it ever okay to tell a lie?

- What's the worst thing you ever did to a friend? What's the best thing?

Okay, okay! That's it for now. I'm sure you'll dream up a zillion more ideas on your own anyway. That's how it works — one great idea leads to another great idea . . . just like one great friend leads to another great friend. That's what led me to you, right?

In case I haven't said it enough (drumroll, please): YOU ROCK. So will your party!

Your sleepover friend forever,

48

The END